Testimony of Secretary Ernest Moniz
U.S. Department of Energy
Before the
Subcommittee on Energy and Power
Committee on Energy and Commerce
U.S. House of Representatives
March 2, 2016

Chairman Whitfield, Ranking Member Rush, and Members of the Subcommittee, thank you for the opportunity to appear before you today to discuss the Department of Energy's (DOE) Budget Request for fiscal year (FY) 2017. I appreciate the opportunity to discuss how the Budget Request advances the Department of Energy's missions.

Advancing Nuclear Security, Science & Energy, and Environmental Cleanup

The Department of Energy requests $32.5 billion for FY 2017, an increase of $2.9 billion from the FY 2016 enacted level of $29.6 billion. The FY 2017 Budget Request consists of $30.2 billion in discretionary funding—$640 million above the FY 2016 enacted appropriation—and $2.3 billion in new mandatory spending proposals requiring new legislation.

The DOE Budget Request supports a broad portfolio of programs, including support for the National Laboratory system of 17 laboratories to carry out critical responsibilities for America's security and economy in three areas:

- Building the Future through Science and Clean Energy;
- Ensuring Nuclear Security; and
- Organizing, Managing and Modernizing the Department to Better Achieve its Enduring Missions.

Underpinning all of these priorities is stewardship of the Department as a science and technology powerhouse, with an unparalleled network of national laboratories, harnessing innovation to successfully address national security, create jobs and increase economic prosperity, boost manufacturing competitiveness, mitigate and adapt to climate change, and enhance energy security.

Energy has been an important driver for recent U.S. economic growth, due to expanded domestic energy production and reduced petroleum imports; increased energy efficiency and productivity; and significant cost reduction and expanded market application of a variety of clean energy generation and energy-efficient industrial, commercial and consumer energy products. DOE has advanced this technology-based energy revolution by supporting the scientific foundations of energy sciences and technology, clean energy and manufacturing technological innovation, early commercial demonstration and deployments, and new technologies and standards to enhance end use energy efficiency. For example, because of DOE technology successes, favorable policies, and other factors, the cost of utility-scale photovoltaic solar power fell 59 percent and power purchase agreements for wind power fell 66 percent from 2008 to 2014. Yet work remains to enhance energy security and U.S. clean energy competitiveness while enabling global climate goals.

The DOE FY 2017 Budget Request includes a programmatic level of $12.9 billion for energy, science, and related programs, an increase of $2.8 billion from the FY 2016 enacted level. The FY 2017 Budget includes $11.3 billion in discretionary funding—$1.2 billion above FY 2016—and $1.6 billion in mandatory spending proposals to support increased investment in leading-edge science and technology; new research facilities to advance the frontiers of science; advanced manufacturing institutes; implementation of the Administration's strategy for nuclear waste management; and crosscutting initiatives to further technological innovation using an enterprise-wide approach to research efforts. The Budget Request takes steps to implement recommendations from the first installment of the Quadrennial Energy Review (QER), released in 2015, to strengthen U.S. energy infrastructures and enhance our collective energy security.

The Request supports ongoing implementation of the President's Climate Action Plan and builds on the systems-based analysis of the Quadrennial Technology Review (QTR) released in 2015. The FY 2017 Budget Request also takes a significant first step toward fulfilling the United States' pledge to seek to double federal clean energy research and development investment over the next five years as part of Mission Innovation, an initiative launched by the U.S. and 19 other countries to accelerate widespread clean energy technology innovation and cost reduction. The Request provides a total of $5.86 billion in discretionary funding for clean energy activities that span the full range of research and development from use-inspired basic research to demonstration, representing an increase in discretionary funding of over 21 percent above the FY 2016 baseline of $4.82 billion. DOE's funding is 76 percent of the $7.7 billion government-wide Mission Innovation investment in FY 2017.

The FY 2017 Budget Request also includes mandatory funding for clean energy R&D that complements activities supported by discretionary funding. The Request includes $150 million in mandatory funding for the Advanced Research Projects Agency—Energy (ARPA-E) as part of the ARPA-E Trust proposal that seeks $1.85 billion in mandatory funding over five years to reliably increase the program's transformational clean energy technology R&D. In addition, as part of the $1.3 billion mandatory proposal for the DOE portion of the Administration's 21st Century Clean Transportation Plan, the Request includes $500 million in FY 2017 to scale-up clean transportation R&D through initiatives to accelerate cutting the cost of battery technology; advance the next generation of low carbon biofuels, in particular for intermodal freight and fleets; and establish a mobility systems integration facility to investigate systems level energy implications of vehicle connectivity and automation.

The FY 2017 Budget Request provides a programmatic level of $12.9 billion for the National Nuclear Security Administration (NNSA), $357 million above the FY 2016 enacted level, to support DOE's nuclear security responsibilities. The Budget Request includes funding to maintain a safe, secure, and effective nuclear deterrent without underground nuclear explosive testing, including life extension programs for major weapons systems and modernization of the Nation's research and production infrastructure.

The Request also ensures that the United States is ready to respond to nuclear and radiological incidents at home and abroad and supports programs that reduce the threats of nuclear proliferation globally, including supporting implementation and monitoring of the Joint Comprehensive Plan of Action with Iran to verifiably prevent Iran from obtaining nuclear weapons. Finally, DOE's Request for nuclear security supports activities that provide safe and effective propulsion for the U.S. nuclear Navy.

The FY 2017 Budget Request includes $6.8 billion for Departmental management and performance programs, including environmental cleanup programs to meet the nation's Manhattan Project and Cold War legacy responsibilities. The Request includes $6.1 billion, which includes $5.4 billion in discretionary funding and proposes $674 million in mandatory spending from the United States Enrichment Corporation Fund, to uphold the U.S. Government's commitment to states and communities to remediate the environmental legacy of over six decades of nuclear weapons and nuclear research, development, and production. The Request supports major management reforms, including new project oversight, assessment, and cost estimation initiatives as part of ongoing efforts to strengthen effective project and program management across the enterprise. The Request also supports continued implementation of a new and improved Human Resource Management service delivery business model and efforts to improve information technology management and further strengthen cybersecurity.

Science and Energy

The FY 2017 Budget Request provides a programmatic level of $12.9 billion for science, energy, and related programs, which is $2.8 billion above the FY 2016 enacted level and includes $11.3 billion in discretionary funding and $1.6 billion in mandatory spending. The Department's science and energy programs invest in all stages of innovation across a diverse portfolio of clean energy technologies to enhance economic competitiveness in a low-carbon world and secure America's long-term energy security. The Request takes the first step in fulfilling the U.S. Government's pledge to Mission Innovation, an unprecedented global initiative across 20 nations to double public clean energy research and development (R&D), in conjunction with commitments for private investments led by a coalition of 28 private investors from ten countries. The Request also continues to implement the President's Climate Action Plan through the development and deployment of clean energy technologies that reduce carbon pollution. Following COP-21, these investments will be a critical next step in enabling the transition to a low carbon energy future through innovation and cost reduction.

The FY 2017 Budget Request sustains DOE's role as the largest federal sponsor of basic research in the physical sciences and constructs and operates cutting-edge scientific user facilities at the National Laboratories to maintain the nation's preeminence in science and innovation. The Request supports transformational R&D in critical technology areas, including advanced manufacturing, renewable energy, sustainable transportation, energy efficiency, electricity grid modernization, advanced nuclear reactors, and fossil energy with carbon capture and storage. The Request builds on the analytical foundation provided by the Department's 2015 Quadrennial Technology Review (QTR), as well as the recommendations of the 2015 Quadrennial Energy Review (QER), by funding measures to strengthen U.S. energy infrastructures and enhance our collective energy security posture.

Mission Innovation: Enabling a Clean Energy Future

The President's FY 2017 Budget Request takes a significant first step toward fulfilling the U.S. pledge to seek to double federal clean energy research and development investment over the next five years as part of Mission Innovation, an initiative launched by the U.S. and 19 other countries to accelerate widespread clean energy technology innovation and cost reduction. It is a widely-shared view that innovation is essential for economic growth by providing affordable and reliable energy for everyone, is critical for energy security, enhances U.S. competitiveness, and is the key to a transition to a clean energy future. Each of the 20 participating countries, which together represent over 80 percent of global governmental clean energy research and development, will seek to double its governmental investment in clean energy research and development over five years. While each country will determine its own doubling plan and portfolio, the collection of countries will provide new opportunities for synergies and collaboration.

The need for a substantial investment in clean energy research and development is clear. Many studies have examined the contribution of technological innovation to U.S. economic growth. In 2010, the American Energy Innovation Council, comprised of Chief Executive Officers from multiple industries, called for the tripling of energy research and development, citing the need for a dramatic expansion of the energy innovation pipeline to meet critical national priorities. Another report that same year from the President's Council of Advisors on Science and Technology also recommended accelerating the pace of technology innovation to meet economic competitiveness, environmental and energy security needs. The need for greater regional innovation efforts was highlighted in a 2012 National Research Council report calling for the establishment of regional innovation cluster initiatives that build upon existing knowledge clusters and comparative strengths of a geographic region.

The President's FY 2017 Budget takes a significant first step toward fulfilling the U.S. pledge to seek to double federal clean energy research and development investment over the next 5 years by providing $7.7 billion across 12 federal agencies, with DOE responsible for approximately 76 percent of that government-wide total. The DOE FY 2017 Request provides a total of $5.86 billion in discretionary funding for clean energy research and development. This funding represents an increase of over 21 percent above the FY 2016 baseline of $4.82 billion of appropriated funds.

The Budget supports clean energy activities that span the innovation spectrum from use-inspired basic research to demonstration, and encompasses all clean energy technologies, including renewable energy, energy efficiency, sustainable transportation, nuclear energy, fossil energy, and the electricity grid of the future. The DOE program components supporting Mission Innovation include elements of use-inspired basic research sponsored by the Office of Science, ARPA-E and portions of the applied energy programs that support clean energy research, development, and demonstration activities. Overall, programs supporting Mission Innovation comprise slightly more than half of the total President's FY 2017 Budget Request for science and energy, including ARPA-E.

The increased investments proposed in the FY 2017 Budget support a broad-based strategy for accelerating the innovation process. The strategy emphasizes investments strategically targeted to support innovative platforms for early stage research and technology development, as well as development and demonstration activities that target cost-reduction and advance transformational concepts that can achieve meaningful scale. For example, the President's FY 2017 Budget supports an expansion of promising existing programs, such as Energy Frontier Research Centers, ARPA-E, Clean Energy Manufacturing Institutes, the BioEnergy Research Centers, SuperTruck II, and advanced carbon capture technology pilot projects. The FY 2017 Budget also supports new initiatives, such as $110 million to establish regional clean energy innovation partnerships, $45 million to expand

R&D collaborations between innovators and small businesses and the DOE National Laboratories, and an advanced materials crosscutting initiative.

The President's FY 2017 Budget also includes mandatory funding for clean energy R&D that complements activities supported by discretionary funding. The FY 2017 Budget Request includes $150 million in mandatory funding for ARPA-E as part of the ARPA-E Trust proposal for $1.85 billion in new mandatory spending authority over five years. The mandatory spending authority will complement annual appropriations by enabling ARPA-E to support projects of a different character than can otherwise be funded under the current program. For example, the mandatory funding will support projects that are larger in scale and address more complex energy challenges that have large transformative potential. As part of the Administration's 21st Century Clean Transportation Plan, the President's FY 2017 Budget Request also includes $500 million in mandatory funding at DOE in FY 2017 to scale-up clean transportation R&D through initiatives to accelerate cutting the cost of battery technology; advance the next generation of low-carbon biofuels, in particular for intermodal freight and fleets; and establish a smart mobility research center to investigate systems level energy implications of vehicle connectivity and automation.

Mission Innovation investments will be leveraged by private capital that drives innovation and clean energy deployment. The initiative is complemented by a separate private sector-led effort, the Breakthrough Energy Coalition (Coalition), as increased government investment, while necessary, is insufficient by itself. This parallel initiative includes over 28 investors from 10 countries and will supplement the large and growing private sector investment in commercialization of clean energy technologies by targeting new investments at an earlier stage of the innovation cycle and managing these investments through the completion of the innovation process, including the formation of new companies and the commercial introduction of new products and processes. The Coalition will be investing in technologies and projects originating in the Mission Innovation participating countries.

Together, these initiatives will drive innovation essential for economic growth enabled by affordable and reliable energy, for energy security, for U.S. competitiveness, and for a transition to a low carbon energy future.

Integrating Science and Energy Programs across the DOE Enterprise

The FY 2017 Budget Request further strengthens DOE and its national missions by fully integrating across its science and energy programs, and across the DOE enterprise with the national laboratories as strategic partners.

DOE has continued to strengthen and institutionalize its strategic relationship with the National Laboratories through organizations and forums such as the Laboratory Policy Council, the Laboratory Operations Board, and the annual National Laboratories Big Ideas summits, which convene DOE and the Laboratories on a regular basis. DOE is sustaining this strategic partnership through these ongoing collaborations and through new efforts, such as a comprehensive report on the National Laboratories. The Request also outlines how DOE will implement recommendations of the Secretary of Energy Advisory Board (SEAB) taskforce on the national laboratories and the Commission to Review the Effectiveness of the National Energy Laboratories (CRENEL). Last week, the Department submitted its detailed response to the final CRENEL report that addresses the Commission's findings and recommendations.

The FY 2017 Budget also supports DOE's crosscutting initiatives that leverage the science, technology, and engineering capabilities across programs and National Laboratory partners. DOE first proposed the crosscutting initiatives in FY 2015 to enhance enterprise-wide planning and improve collaboration across organization boundaries for key science and technology areas with impact across DOE's missions. Each crosscutting initiative reflects a comprehensive and integrated work plan to optimize programmatic objectives and efficiently allocate resources. The crosscutting initiatives help bolster DOE's efforts to institutionalize enhanced program management and coordination across program offices, while accelerating progress on key national priorities.

DOE has two years of experience with integrated planning and program management across program offices, enabling accelerated progress on key national priorities. The FY 2015 and FY 2016 appropriations have provided DOE with funding for the crosscutting initiatives, including $1.1 billion in FY 2016 coordinated across all three Under Secretaries. Moving forward, the FY 2017 Budget Request continues six existing crosscutting initiatives, and proposes a new initiative, Advanced Materials for Energy Innovation. Together, the initiatives closely coordinate the $1.5 billion request, a $330 million increase, in crosscutting R&D across the enterprise in seven technology areas:

- Electricity grid technology modernization accelerates the development of the technologies and tools to enable modernization of the grid to support U.S. economic growth, environmental quality and security objectives.
- Subsurface science, technology, and engineering coordinates efforts to develop next-generation technologies for energy generation, storage, and disposal applications through mastery of the subsurface, with a science-based focus on advanced imaging of geophysical and geochemical signals.
- Supercritical carbon dioxide technology enables large-scale commercialization of the supercritical carbon dioxide (sCO2) power cycle, which has the potential for higher thermal efficiencies with lower capital cost compared to steam-based power systems and can provide significant benefits for electric power generation, including reducing the costs of carbon capture and storage.
- Energy-water nexus accelerates the Nation's transition to more resilient and sustainable coupled energy-water systems, including a new effort on desalination technology and regional data, modeling and analysis test beds.
- Exascale computing, a joint Science-NNSA collaboration, significantly accelerates the development and deployment of capable exascale computing systems, applications and software infrastructure to meet national security needs and to provide next-generation tools for scientific discovery;
- Cybersecurity protects the Department of Energy enterprise from a range of cyber threats and improves cybersecurity in the electric power and oil and natural gas subsectors; and
- Advanced materials for energy innovations, which have the potential to revolutionize entire industries by employing advanced synthesis, modeling, and characterization to accelerate and reduce the cost of materials qualification in a wide variety of clean energy applications.

Science: Providing the Backbone for Discovery and Innovation

DOE's Office of Science is the largest federal sponsor of basic research in the physical sciences, supporting more than 24,000 investigators at over 300 U.S. academic institutions and the DOE laboratories. The Office of Science provides the backbone for discovery and innovation, especially in the physical sciences, for America's research community.

The FY 2017 Budget Request provides $5.67 billion for Science, $325 million above the FY 2016 enacted level, to lead basic research in the physical sciences and develop and operate cutting-edge scientific user facilities while strengthening the connection between advances in fundamental science and technology innovation. The FY 2017 Budget Request includes a proposal for $100 million in mandatory funding for university grants that will be made available through a competitive, merit-based review of proposals solicited from and provided by the university community in the Office of Science mission areas.

The Budget Request provides major increases for advanced scientific computing research, basic energy sciences, and biological and environmental research, and funding to operate the Office of Science's scientific user facilities at optimal levels in support of more than 31,000 researchers from universities, national laboratories, industry, and international partners.

Sustaining Leading-Edge Discovery Science

The FY 2017 Budget Request sustains leading-edge discovery science through support for the High Energy Physics and Nuclear Physics programs, a 14% increase in investments in Scientific Laboratories Infrastructure, and the new $100 million mandatory proposal for university grants.

In these discovery science programs, Office of Science has contributed to many major recent accomplishments, including collaborating with two international experiments that led to the Nobel Prize in physics for discovering oscillations in neutrinos (fundamental building blocks of our universe that remain poorly understood); contributing to the discovery of three of the four new superheavy elements in the periodic table; opening the most advanced storage-ring-based light source facility, the National Synchrotron Light Source II (NSLS-II); and continuing effective execution of major ongoing science construction projects—the Linac Coherent Light Source II (LCLS-II) and the Facility for Rare Isotope Beams (FRIB)—on schedule and within budget.

For High Energy Physics, the request provides $818 million, $23 million above the FY 2016 enacted level, to understand how the universe works at its most fundamental level by discovering the most elementary constituents of matter and energy, probing the interactions among them, and exploring the basic nature of space and time. The Request implements activities and projects based on the High Energy Physics Advisory Panel (HEPAP) May 2014 strategic plan, including $45 million, an increase of $19 million, to support design for a reconfigured international Long Baseline Neutrino Facility hosted at Fermilab and initial construction for the Deep Underground Neutrino Experiment in South Dakota.

For Nuclear Physics research, the Budget includes $636 million, $19 million above the FY 2016 enacted level, to discover, explore, and understand nuclear matter in a variety of different forms, including continued construction of the Facility for Rare Isotope Beams (FRIB).

Expanding Use-Inspired Research

The Office of Science funds basic science programs that support use-inspired research towards energy and other applications. The Budget Request provides funding to increase operation of the National Laboratory user facilities to optimal levels to accommodate increases in Mission Innovation work. The Request also expands investments in foundations for key technology crosscutting areas, including advanced materials, the subsurface, and the energy-water nexus.

The FY 2017 Budget Request includes $1.94 billion for Basic Energy Sciences, $88 million above the FY 2016 enacted level, to provide the foundations for new energy technologies, to mitigate the environmental impacts of energy use, and to support DOE missions in energy, environment, and national security by understanding, predicting, and ultimately controlling matter and energy. The Budget Request provides $143 million, an increase of $33 million, to initiate five new Energy Frontier Research Centers (EFRCs) and continue to support the existing EFRCs.

The Request provides $662 million for Biological and Environmental Research, $53 million above the FY 2016 enacted level, to support fundamental research and scientific user facilities to achieve a predictive understanding of complex biological, climatic, and environmental systems for a secure and sustainable energy future, including an expanded focus on regional energy-water systems. The Request provides $90 million, a $15 million increase, to expand technology transfer activities during the last year of a ten-year program at the three existing Bioenergy Research Centers (BRC). The Request also includes $10 million for a new initiative in microbiome research that builds on the Department's experience in fundamental genomic science of plants and microbes to understand the fundamental principles governing microbiome interactions in diverse environments.

For Fusion Energy Sciences, the FY 2017 Budget Request includes $398 million, $40 million below FY 2016. The Request will continue to support research to understand the behavior of matter at high temperatures and densities and to develop fusion as a future energy source. The Budget Request also includes $125 million for the U.S. contribution to the ITER project, a major fusion research facility being constructed by an international partnership of seven governments. The Department submitted in mid-February an interim report to Congress on the status of ITER, and we are scheduled to deliver a report in early May with recommendations related to the project.

Investing in High Performance Computing to Support Frontier Science

The Budget Request provides $663 million for Advanced Scientific Computing Research (ASCR), $42 million above the FY 2016 enacted level, to support research in advanced computation, applied mathematics, computer science and networking, as well as development and operation of high-performance computing facilities.

Under this program, DOE has implemented the President's Executive Order on National Strategic Computing Initiative through a multi-year joint program between the Office of Science and NNSA to achieve capable exascale computing. As part of the President's national initiative, DOE announced a $200 million supercomputer award for Argonne National Laboratory, part of a joint

Collaboration of Oak Ridge, Argonne, and Lawrence Livermore (CORAL) initiative to develop supercomputers that will be five to seven times more powerful than today's fastest systems in the United States.

The FY 2017 Budget includes $190 million across three Office of Science programs, joined by $95 million in NNSA, to accelerate development of capable exascale computing systems with a thousand-fold improvement in performance over current high-performance computers in support of the President's National Strategic Computing Initiative. Within the Request, the Office of Science will transition exascale funding to a formal Exascale Computing Project, which will follow DOE project management guidelines under DOE Order 413.3b. The Budget also provides $46 million to re-compete the SciDAC partnerships, with new activities to include accelerating the development of clean energy technologies.

The Request funds research on high-performance computing applications unique to the biomedical research community, including $9 million for the President's BRAIN Initiative, in close coordination with the National Institutes of Health. This funding will bring to bear DOE national laboratory capabilities in big data analytics, modeling and simulation and machine learning to support biomedical research challenges in cancer and BRAIN. In other DOE science programs, the Request also enables development of accelerator applications, including advanced proton and ion beams for the treatment of cancer, in coordination with NIH.

Energy Research, Development, Demonstration, and Deployment

The FY 2017 Budget Request provides a programmatic level of $6.6 billion for energy research, development, demonstration, and deployment activities, of which $5.2 billion is discretionary funding—an increase of $928 million from FY 2016. The Request supports a diverse portfolio of energy technologies, including renewable electricity, energy efficiency and advanced manufacturing, sustainable transportation, fossil energy, nuclear energy, and a modernized grid.

DOE recently completed the 2015 Quadrennial Technology Review (QTR), a systems-based analytical foundation to inform program research priorities across DOE's entire portfolio of energy and science programs by examining the most promising research, development, demonstration, and deployment (RDD&D) opportunities across energy technologies to effectively address the nation's energy needs. The 2015 QTR builds upon the first QTR conducted in 2011 by describing the nation's energy landscape and the dramatic changes that have taken place over the last four years and identifying the RDD&D activities, opportunities, and pathways forward to help address our national energy challenges.

Improving Cost and Performance of Renewable Electricity Technologies

DOE's FY 2017 Budget Request for Energy Efficiency and Renewable Energy (EERE) invests $621 million in renewable energy generation technologies, an increase of $143 million from FY 2016. Innovations, favorable policies, and other factors have led to significant cost and performance improvements across the spectrum of renewable energy technologies, as documented in Revolution…Now[1] report. To name a few examples, the cost of utility-scale photovoltaic solar power fell 59 percent from $5.70 per watt in 2008 to $2.34 per watt in 2014; power purchase agreements for wind power fell 66 percent from 7 cents per kilowatt-hour in 2008 to 2.4 cents per kilowatt-hour in 2014; and the median installed price of residential photovoltaic solar power fell 51 percent from $8.80 per watt in 2008 to $4.30 per watt in 2014.

The Request provides $285M, an increase of $44M, to continue the SunShot Initiative on a path to achieve solar cost parity without subsidies by 2020. The Budget includes $156 million for Wind Energy, an increase of $61 million, to continue efforts to achieve a 16.7 cents per kilowatt-hour cost target for offshore wind by 2020, including $30 million for offshore wind demonstration projects and $25 million to establish an Offshore Wind R&D Consortium.

The Budget Request provides just under $100 million, $29 million above FY 2016, for geothermal technologies, including $35 million to select the final site and team for FORGE, a field laboratory for enhanced geothermal systems, beginning with a down-selection from five to three teams.

The Request also provides $80 million for water power technologies, a $10 million increase, including $25 million to continue the HydroNEXT initiative focusing on innovative, low-cost water diversion technologies to enable new stream reach hydropower, to progress to a cost target of 10.9 cents per kilowatt-hour by 2020

---

[1] http://energy.gov/sites/prod/files/2015/11/f27/Revolution-Now-11132015.pdf

from small, low-head new stream developments. The Request also includes $55 million, $11 million above FY 2016, to support marine and hydrokinetic technologies, including a grid-connected open-water test facility and development of concepts for revolutionary wave-energy converters.

Improving Energy Efficiency and Advanced Manufacturing Technologies

The FY 2017 Budget for EERE includes $919 million, $198 million above FY 2016, to invest in the development of manufacturing technologies and enhanced energy efficiency in our homes, buildings and industries.

In 2015, DOE issued 13 final energy efficiency standards as part of the Administration's goal to reduce carbon pollution. Standards issued to date will achieve cumulative reduction of 2.3 billion metric tons cumulatively by 2030. To accelerate innovation in energy efficiency and manufacturing programs, DOE continues to fund R&D at the Manufacturing Demonstration Facility, funds continuing work at the Critical Materials Institute, and is implementing a total of five Clean Energy Manufacturing Institutes in FY 2016 as part of the National Network for Manufacturing Innovation.

The FY 2017 Budget Request provides $14 million in EERE for the sixth Clean Energy Manufacturing Institute and $25 million to establish a new Energy-Water Desalination Hub to serve as a focal point for enabling technologies for de-energizing, de-carbonizing, and reducing the cost of desalination.

The FY 2017 Budget provides $169 million, an increase of $83 million, for emerging technologies that reduce building energy consumption, including $40 million for an R&D effort to transition to refrigerant technologies with low global warming potential, and the Budget provides $15 million for a new metropolitan systems initiative to use new sensing, communication and computation capabilities to create actionable information for decision-makers on clean energy issues. The Request also provides $230 million, an increase of $15 million, to support weatherization retrofits to approximately 35,700 low-income homes nationwide; $70 million to support state energy offices; and $26 million for a new Cities, Counties, and Communities Energy Program to provide support to local governments, public housing authorities, non-profits and other stakeholders to catalyze more extensive clean energy investments in revitalization efforts.

Advancing Sustainable Transportation

The FY 2017 Budget provides $853 million in discretionary funding, $217 million above FY 2016, for sustainable transportation including vehicle, bioenergy, and hydrogen and fuel cells technologies.

In FY 2016, DOE will achieve high-volume modeled costs for batteries of $250 per kilowatt-hour—down from the current cost of $289 per kilowatt-hour—towards a goal of $125 per kilowatt-hour in 2022 as part of the EV Everywhere Grand Challenge. EERE will initiate SuperTruck II, with up to four new competitively awarded projects to improve freight efficiency of heavy-duty vehicles. The programs will achieve at least 1.15 billion gallons per year savings from Clean Cities' initiatives and fund, with the Departments of Agriculture and Defense, three commercial-scale biorefineries to produce military specification drop-in fuels.

The FY 2107 Budget includes $469 million for vehicle technologies, $159 million above FY 2016, including $60 million to fully fund the multi-year SuperTruck II program to double freight truck efficiency by 2020, and $283 million, an increase of $102 million, for continuing the EV Everywhere program to enable domestic production of plug-in electric vehicles that are as affordable and convenient as gasoline vehicles by 2022. The Budget provides $279 million for bioenergy technologies, $54 million above FY 2016, including $52 million to continue R&D efforts on converting cellulosic and algal-based feedstocks to bio-based gasoline and diesel.

The FY 2107 Budget Request includes an additional $1.3 billion mandatory proposal for DOE to expand investments in low-carbon transportation technologies and fueling infrastructure as part of the Administration's 21st Century Clean Transportation Plan. The proposal for DOE would invest $500 million in clean transportation R&D, $750 million in regional fueling infrastructures for low-carbon fuels, and $85 million in the deployment of clean vehicle fleets for local governments and first responders.

Crosscutting Innovation Initiatives for Energy

The Request for EERE includes $215 million for new crosscutting innovation initiatives to enable the acceleration of clean energy innovation and commercialization in the United States by strengthening regional clean energy innovation ecosystems, accelerating next-generation clean energy technology pathways, and encouraging clean energy innovation and commercialization collaborations between our National Laboratories and American entrepreneurs.

The Request includes $110 million to support Regional Energy Innovation Partnerships, a new competition to establish regionally-focused clean energy innovation partnerships around the country. These regionally focused and directed partnerships will support regionally relevant technology-neutral clean energy RD&D needs and opportunities to support accelerated clean energy technology commercialization, economic development, and manufacturing.

The FY 2017 Budget Request also includes $60 million for a Next-Generation Innovation funding opportunity to accelerate next-generation clean energy technology pathways by supporting research, development, and demonstration (RD&D) projects with the greatest potential to change the trajectory of EERE core program technology pathways. The Request includes $20 million for a new Small Business Partnerships program to competitively provide technology RD&D resources to small businesses through the DOE's National Labs to support their efforts to commercialize promising new clean energy. The Request also includes $25 million for Energy Technology Innovation Accelerators that will leverage the technical assets and facilities of the National Laboratories to enable American entrepreneurs to conduct RD&D that leads to the creation of new clean energy businesses.

Expanding Transformational ARPA-E Programs

The FY 2017 Budget Request provides $500 million for the Advanced Research Projects Agency—Energy (ARPA-E), which fills a unique role in identifying scientific discoveries and cutting-edge inventions and accelerating their translation into technological innovations. Of this, $350 million is requested in discretionary funding, $59 million above the FY 2016 enacted level, to fund additional early-stage innovative programs as well as to exploit the technological opportunities developed in previous ARPA-E programs.

ARPA-E has achieved considerable results to date. Through early 2015, 141 ARPA-E project teams have completed funded work. Thirty four ARPA-E projects attracted more than $850 million in private sector follow-on funding, and over 30 ARPA-E teams formed new companies. Eight companies had commercial sales of new products resulting from ARPA-E projects, and more than 37 ARPA-E projects partnered with other government entities for further development. At the annual ARPA-E Summit being held this week, we will be announcing updated numbers demonstrating further success with ARPA-E's portfolio of projects.

The FY 2017 Budget Request will expand support for the current core portfolio of early stage innovation programs, including the release of 7-8 funding opportunity announcements (FOA) for new focused technology programs. Possible areas of focus for these FOAs include advanced sensors and analytics for energy management and improved light metals production to transform vehicle light-weighting. The Request also supports the continuation of the Innovative Development In Energy-Related Applied Science (IDEAS) FOA, which provides a continuing opportunity for the rapid support of early-stage applied research to explore innovative new concepts with the potential for transformational and disruptive changes in energy technology. Across all activities, ARPA-E will continue to emphasize supporting commercial readiness for highly successful projects.

In addition, the FY 2017 Budget Request includes a new legislative proposal for the Advanced Research Projects Agency—Energy Trust, which provides $150 million in FY 2017 and a total of $1.85 billion in mandatory funds over five years to add a new focus on innovative systems level development that will deliver larger, more rapid benefits to the economic, environmental, and energy security of the United States. These projects are of a different character than can otherwise be funded with annual discretionary appropriations, and include, for example, potentially transformative technologies facing significant technical challenges in scale-up, projects that integrate multiple technical advances, and projects that address system-level transformation of energy cycles. The proposed new mandatory spending authority will accelerate transformational changes on energy systems.

Revitalizing the Nuclear Fuel Cycle

The FY 2017 Budget Request provides $994 million for Nuclear Energy, $8 million above the FY 2016 enacted level, to help meet energy security, proliferation resistance, and climate goals. These funds will to support the diverse civilian nuclear energy programs of the U.S. Government, leading federal efforts to research and develop nuclear energy technologies, including generation, safety, waste storage and management, and security technologies.

In 2015, the program funded the second 5-year program of the Consortium for Advanced Simulation of Light Water Reactors (CASL) Hub and new R&D programs for two advanced reactor technologies, pebble bed and chloride fast reactors. The FY 2017 Budget Request provides $73.5 million for ongoing R&D in advanced reactor technologies and continued R&D support for light water reactors (LWR), $59 million for accident tolerant fuels, and $35 million for LWR sustainability. Funding is also requested to continue the GAIN initiative to provide streamlined access for advanced reactor developers to access the world-class nuclear energy R&D capabilities at the national laboratories. The Request includes $89.6 million to continue funding for a cost-shared cooperative agreement for licensing technical support of a small modular reactor design, including support for a small modular reactor design (SMR) certification application to the Nuclear Regulatory Commission (NRC) by December 2016, for application review by the NRC, and to continue development of permit and license applications for the first domestic SMR deployments.

In 2015, DOE's nuclear energy program awarded a contract for a deep borehole field characterization test and issued an Invitation for Public Comment to initiate the dialogue on a consent-based siting process to support a consolidated commercial used fuel storage, a permanent repository and a separate disposal path for defense waste. The Request continues implementation of the Administration's Strategy for the Management and Disposal of Used Nuclear Fuel and High Level Radioactive Waste by providing $76.3 million, an increase of $53.8 million, for integrated waste management system activities in the areas of transportation, storage, disposal, and consent-based siting. The Request includes $39.4 million for consent-based siting, including $25 million for grants to states, Tribes, and local governments. The Request also includes $26 million to complete characterization of a field test borehole and to initiate drilling.

Enabling Fossil Energy to Compete in a Low-Carbon Energy Future

The Budget Request provides $600 million for Fossil Energy Research and Development ($240 million of which is available through repurposing of prior-year balances), $32 million below the FY 2016 enacted level, to advance research and development in carbon capture and storage, advanced energy systems, cross-cutting areas, and fuel supply impact mitigation.

In FY 2016, DOE is reaching several milestones in its support for carbon capture, utilization and storage (CCUS). DOE completed funding of two large-scale industrial CCUS projects that are in operation to demonstrate the feasibility and economics of carbon capture on an ethanol facility and the technology for carbon capture on a hydrogen production unit. Through cost-shared cooperative agreements, DOE is supporting two large-scale, coal-based CCUS demonstration projects utilizing coal gasification and post-combustion carbon capture technologies, with construction to be completed in 2016.

The FY 2017 Budget Request provides $50 million, an increase of $20M, to support initial construction of three large-scale pilot projects of advanced, second generation, post combustion carbon capture technologies critical to reducing cost and increasing efficiency of CCUS technologies. The Request includes $24 million to initiate the design and construction of a supercritical carbon dioxide (CO_2) pilot plant test facility at the 10 megawatt-electric (MWe) scale, and $31 million to initiate design of a natural gas combined cycle (NGCC) demonstration facility employing CCUS technology.

The budget includes the reallocation of funding from CCUS demonstration projects that have not reached financial close to fund other projects and new initiatives, including the use of $240 million in prior-year balances.

Also in support of CCUS technologies, the President's FY 2017 Budget Request makes available $5 billion in proposed investment and sequestration tax credits for qualified commercial CCUS projects. These tax credits are complemented by an existing $8.5 billion available through DOE's loan guarantees for advanced fossil energy projects to help provide critical financing to support new or significantly improved advanced fossil energy projects, and additional mixed-use authority for loan guarantees in the FY 2017 Budget that can be used for advanced fossil and other technologies.

Expanding Technology Commercialization and Deployment

Significant advances have been made in recent years in commercializing and deploying innovative technologies have been made. In 2015, DOE received 30 out of 100 R&D Magazine awards for outstanding technology developments with promising commercial potential, and the Administration announced new investment commitments from the institutional investment community of $4 billion for deployment of clean energy technologies. The renewable energy production tax credits were also extended by the Congress in December 2015.

To expand the commercial impact of DOE's portfolio of research, development, demonstration, and deployment activities in the short, medium and long term, DOE established the Office of Technology Transitions (OTT) in 2015 to oversee and advance DOE's technology transfer mission. The FY 2017 Budget Request provides $8.4 million for the OTT to expand the commercial impact of the DOE portfolio of activities. The Request provides for coordination of technology-to-market activities across the Department and the implementation of the Technology Commercialization Fund (TCF), approximately $20 million in FY 2017, to catalyze seed-stage funding for collaborations with private sector partners on high potential energy technologies at the National Laboratories. The Budget Request for OTT also supports implementation of the Clean Energy Investment Center (CEIC) to provide better information on investable opportunities resulting from DOE R&D.

DOE's Loan Programs Office, in its role accelerating the domestic commercial deployment of innovative and advanced clean energy technologies, has maintained a financially sound portfolio of loans and loan guarantees. The $32 billion portfolio of loans, loan guarantees, and conditional commitments has been supported by $18 billion in financing from project sponsors, and 22 projects with DOE-backed loans and loan guarantees have now successfully completed construction and initiated operation. DOE has received new applications seeking over $20 billion in Advanced Technology Vehicles Manufacturing (ATVM) and Title XVII loans and loan guarantees

The FY 2017 Budget Request supports the Department's continued oversight of more than $30 billion in loans, loan guarantees, and conditional commitments, as well as its administration of remaining loan and loan guarantee authority to finance projects in the areas of advanced nuclear energy, renewable energy and efficient energy, advanced fossil energy, and advanced technology vehicles manufacturing. The FY 2017 Request also proposes an additional $4 billion of mixed-use loan guarantee authority for innovative energy projects that reduce greenhouse gas emissions.

The FY 2017 Request also includes $23 million for the Office of Indian Energy, $7 million above the FY 2016 enacted level, to support DOE's partnership with the Department of the Interior to address the need for clean, sustainable energy systems on Indian lands through expanded technical assistance and grant programs.

Enabling Secure, Modern, and Resilient Energy Infrastructures

The Department's energy programs also support a secure, modern and resilient energy infrastructure, including for the electric power grid. The FY 2017 Budget Request continues a focus on this mission by providing increased investments in the electricity grid of the future.

DOE has also taken major steps in implementing the Grid Modernization Initiative, supported by a Grid Modernization National Laboratory Consortium comprising 400 partners, including the release of DOE's new comprehensive new Grid Modernization Multi-Year Program Plan and the announcement of a $220 million funding opportunity for the National Labs and partners.

The FY 2017 Budget Request includes $262 million for Electricity Delivery and Energy Reliability, $56 million above the FY 2016 enacted level, for grid modernization research to support a smart, resilient electric grid for the 21st century and the storage technology that underpins it, as well as funding critical emergency response and grid physical security capabilities. The Request provides

$14 million to establish a new competitively-selected Grid Clean Energy Manufacturing Innovation Institute as a part of the multi-agency National Network for Manufacturing Innovation, to focus on technologies related to critical metals for grid application, and advances will be broadly applicable in multiple industries and markets.

The Request for Electricity Delivery and Energy Reliability also provides $45 million for energy storage R&D, an increase of $24 million, and $30 million for smart grid R&D. To fortify grid security and resilience, the Request includes $46 million to advance cybersecurity technologies and $18 million for infrastructure security and energy restoration activities. The Request provides $15 million for a new state energy assurance program that supports regional and state activities to continually improve energy assurance plans, improve capabilities to characterize energy sector supply disruptions, communicate among the local, state, regional, federal, and industry partners, and identify gaps for use in energy planning and emergency response training programs. The Request also provides $15 million to launch a new state distribution-level reform program for competitive awards to states to utilize a grid architecture approach to address their system challenges.

The Budget Request also includes $257 million for the Strategic Petroleum Reserve (SPR), $45 million above the FY 2016 enacted level, to increase the system's durability and reliability and ensure operational readiness. The Bipartisan Budget Act of 2015 requires the Department to submit to Congress a Strategic Review of the SPR by May, 2016. The Act also authorized DOE, subject to appropriation, to sell up to $2 billion in SPR oil to fund SPR infrastructure modernization. The results of the SPR Strategic Review will inform SPR infrastructure modernization and shall result in an FY 2017 budget amendment related to SPR modernization.

The FY 2017 Budget Request provides $31 million for Energy Policy and Systems Analysis to continue serving as a focal point for policy coordination within the Department on the formulation, analysis, and implementation of energy policy and related programmatic options and initiatives that could facilitate the transition to a clean and secure energy economy.

EPSA also serves as the Secretariat of the multi-agency Quadrennial Energy Review (QER), and provides systems analysis to support this Administration's initiative. The Administration expects to complete the second installment of the QER in 2016, focused on the electricity sector.

The Budget Request also includes $84 million for the power marketing administrations, including the Western Area, Southeastern, Southwestern, and Bonneville Power Administrations.

Enhancing Collective Energy Security in Global Energy Markets

While DOE's work in global energy security is not a major budgetary issue, it is an important issue for the Nation. DOE has pursued an increased global focus on collective energy security—energy security for the United States and its allies—in the last several years.

For example, as part of this effort and supported by our Office of International Affairs, the G-7 recently reached an agreement to enhance cybersecurity assessments of energy systems. The FY 2017 Budget Request supports DOE's efforts to enhance collective energy security by providing $19 million for the Office of International Affairs, which coordinates the Department's activities to strengthen international energy technology, information and analytical collaborations.

In the area of energy exports, DOE has released a two-part LNG export study for public comment evaluating the impact of increasing LNG exports from 12 billion cubic feet per day (Bcf/d) to 20 Bcf/d. The study will be used in the public interest evaluation of pending applications to export LNG to non-FTA countries. DOE also chaired the International Energy Agency Ministerial resulting in a plan to assess energy security implications of natural gas supply.

Following the North American ministerial in 2014, Canada, Mexico, and the United States have worked together to produce new integrated mapping and information products. The Budget Request for the Energy Information Administration provides $131 million, a $9 million increase, to build upon enhancements like these in carrying out EIA's data collection and analysis mission. The increase will provide greater regional detail and analysis of petroleum data, enhance commercial building energy efficiency data. The Budget will also extend analysis of international data to include Canada-Mexico collaboration and Asia and expand collection of transportation energy consumption data.

Nuclear Security

The President's 2015 National Security Strategy, the 2010 Nuclear Posture Review (NPR), and the ratification of the New Strategic Arms Reduction Treaty underscored the importance of the DOE's nuclear mission and the lasting mandate for DOE to maintain a safe, secure, and effective stockpile for as long as nuclear weapons exist. DOE advances the President's vision to eliminate and secure nuclear material, reduce nuclear stockpiles, and increase global cooperation.

The FY 2017 Budget Request proposes $12.9 billion for the National Nuclear Security Administration (NNSA), $357 million above the FY 2016 enacted level, to invest in our nuclear security by modernizing and maintaining our nuclear security enterprise, refurbishing and extending the life of our nuclear deterrent, reducing the threats of nuclear proliferation, and supporting the safe and reliable operation of our nuclear Navy. As part of an overall focus to modernize nuclear security research and production infrastructure, the overall NNSA budget includes a total of $1.8 billion in proposed infrastructure investments, including $575 million for the new Uranium Processing Facility.

The Request for NNSA includes $413 million for NNSA Federal Salaries and Expenses for the salary, benefits, and support expenses of 1,715 federal full-time equivalents (FTEs) to provide appropriate federal oversight of the nuclear security enterprise responsible for managing and executing NNSA's weapons activities and nonproliferation missions.

Stewardship of the Nuclear Deterrent

August of 2015 marked the 20th anniversary of President Bill Clinton's announcement that the United States would pursue negotiations for the Comprehensive Nuclear-Test-Ban Treaty and maintain the U.S. nuclear arsenal without nuclear explosive tests. This was an important milestone for a science-based Stockpile Stewardship Program that successfully pushed the limits of modern science and engineering to maintain the stockpile without underground nuclear explosive testing.

The FY 2017 Budget Request includes $9.2 billion for Weapons Activities, $396 million above the FY 2016 enacted level, to build on these accomplishments as NNSA sustains a credible and effective nuclear deterrent while continuing to reduce the size of the active stockpile. The Budget Request supports the work, as laid out in the Stockpile Stewardship and Management Plan, of the science-based Stockpile Stewardship Program to ensure a safe, secure and effective nuclear stockpile in the absence of underground nuclear explosive testing through a sustained, long-term research program.

NNSA has achieved major accomplishments in that mission, such as substantial progress on its Life Extension Programs (LEPs), including those for the B61-12, W76-1, W80-4, and W88 Alt 370 with conventional high explosive (CHE) refresh. The Inertial Confinement Fusion Ignition and High Yield Program increased the number of experiments, or "shot rate," at Lawrence Livermore National Laboratory's National Ignition Facility from 191 in 2014 to 356 in 2015. NNSA received the first hardware delivery for Trinity, NNSA's next generation high performance computer, and completed the first subproject for the Uranium Processing Facility, Site Readiness, on time and under budget.

The FY 2017 Request includes $1.3 billion for LEPs and major alterations (Alts), $38 million above FY 2016. In particular, the Request continues timely execution of the B61-12 LEP and the W80-4 LEP. These are the first two steps in implementing the Nuclear Weapons Council-approved "3+2" strategy to consolidate the stockpile to three ballistic missile warheads and two air delivered systems, reducing the number of weapons in the deployed stockpile and simplifying maintenance requirements.

The Request provides $223 million to support completing production of the W76 by 2019 and $616 million to deliver the B61-12 first production unit by 2020. It also supports transitioning the W88 Alt 370 with CHE refresh to Production Engineering in February 2017 with $281 million and provides $220 million, an increase of $25 million, to maintain the schedule of the first production unit for the W80-4 LEP by 2025. The Budget Request also provides $69 million, $17 million above the FY 2016 enacted level, to make progress towards meeting the President's commitment to accelerate dismantlement of retired U. S. nuclear warheads by 20 percent.

The Budget Request for Weapons Activities provides $2.7 billion for Infrastructure and Operations, $443 million above FY 2016. The Request ensures no increase in the backlog of deferred maintenance. The Request will dispose of the Kansas City Bannister Federal Complex, and upgrade aging infrastructure to address safety and programmatic risks, improve productivity, and lower operating costs. The Request for Infrastructure and Operations also provides $575 million, $145 million above FY 2016, to continue the phased approach for constructing the Uranium Processing Facility, including completion of the design and continued construction on approved subprojects. The request also provides $160 million to continue work on the Chemistry and Metallurgy Research Replacement project to support the plutonium strategy.

As part of the Office of Science-NNSA collaboration on the Exascale Computing Initiative, the Budget includes $95 million for exascale computing, $31 million or 48 percent above FY 2016, to develop exascale-class high performance computing to meet the needs for future assessments, LEPs, and stockpile stewardship.

The Request for Weapons Activities also includes $283 million for Secure Transportation Asset, $46 million above FY 2016, to continue asset modernization and workforce capability initiatives including conceptual design and systems prototyping of the new Mobile Guardian Transporter.

Controlling and Eliminating Nuclear Materials Worldwide

The FY 2017 Budget Request includes $1.8 billion for Defense Nuclear Nonproliferation, $132 million below the FY 2016 enacted level, to continue the critical missions of securing or eliminating nuclear and radiological materials worldwide, countering illicit trafficking of these materials, preventing the proliferation of nuclear weapon technologies and expertise, ensuring that the United States remains ready to respond to high consequence nuclear and radiological incidents at home or abroad, and applying technical and policy solutions to solve nonproliferation and arms control challenges around the world. Note that while the overall program level for DNN is down, the programmatic funding level in the FY 2017 Budget Request is roughly flat with FY 2016 due to the availability of prior-year carryover balances and termination of the Mixed-Oxide (MOX) Fuel Fabrication Facility Project.

DOE has taken major steps in the nuclear threat reduction missions. We recently issued the first nonproliferation strategic plan, *Prevent, Counter and Respond—A Strategic Plan to Reduce Global Nuclear Threats*[2], to define and describe our missions.

Supported largely by the DNN program and capabilities, we also provided scientific technical analysis to support the U.S. delegation during the Joint Comprehensive Plan of Action (JCPOA) negotiations. Following finalization of the agreement, twenty nine scientific leaders deeply familiar with nuclear issues (familiar names such as Garwin, Drell, Dyson, Hecker, Richter, and others), focusing on the agreement's nuclear dimensions, wrote to the President: "This is an innovative agreement, with much more stringent constraints than any previously negotiated nonproliferation framework." These experts were referring to aspects of the agreement such as weaponization constraints and bans on nuclear weapons R&D that mark an unprecedented approach to such agreements—and highlight the critical role that DOE plays in providing unparalleled scientific and technical capabilities.

As part of NNSA's goal to minimize and, when possible, eliminates weapons-usable nuclear material around the world, we have also recently completed removal or confirmed disposition of fissile nuclear material, bringing the number of countries free of all highly enriched uranium (HEU) to 28, plus Taiwan. We have also down-blended additional HEU to achieve a cumulative total of 150 metric tons of U.S. excess, weapons-usable HEU.

And in the area of nuclear counterterrorism and incident response, NNSA realigned its counterterrorism and counterproliferation functions to more efficiently respond to nuclear or radiological incidents worldwide and to sustain counterterrorism capabilities through innovative technology and policy-driven solutions. The program continues to train and exercise to strengthen emergency

---

[2] http://nnsa.energy.gov/sites/default/files/NPCR%20Report_FINAL_4-14-15.pdf

preparedness and response capabilities, including nuclear forensics operations, domestically and worldwide.

Looking ahead, the FY 2017 Budget Request will support continued successful execution of the mission to control and eliminate nuclear materials worldwide. NNSA will support the President's fourth and final Nuclear Security Summit in March-April 2016, continuing the President's aim to achieved tangible improvements in the security of nuclear materials and stronger international institutions that support nuclear security.

DOE and its national laboratories will continue to provide technical support to the International Atomic Energy Agency (IAEA), including to implement the JCPOA, and will remain highly engaged in providing training and technologies and other support to support the IAEA. The Request includes $13 million to support implementation of the JCPOA, including $10M to support JCPOA material management activities and $3 million for technical and in-kind support for the U.S. interagency process and the IAEA.

In the area of plutonium disposition, the Budget Request will terminate the Mixed Oxide (MOX) approach and move to a dilute and dispose approach that will be faster and significantly less expensive than the MOX option. Specifically, the FY 2017 Budget Request provides $270 million, $70 million below FY 2016, to terminate the MOX Fuel Fabrication Facility, and an additional $15 million to pursue a dilute and dispose (D&D) approach that will disposition surplus U.S. weapon-grade plutonium by diluting it and disposing of it at a geologic repository. The Department will complete pre-conceptual design for the D&D option and begin conceptual design in late FY 2017.

In other nonproliferation areas, the Request includes $272 million, $37 million above FY 2016, to sustain emergency response and nuclear counterterrorism capabilities that are applied against a wide range of high-consequence nuclear or radiological incidents and threats. It proposes $394 million for the Defense Nuclear Nonproliferation Research and Development program to advance technical capabilities to monitor foreign nuclear weapons program activities, diversion of special nuclear material, and nuclear detonations. The Request provides $341 million for Material Management and Minimization to support HEU and plutonium disposition, the conversion of research reactors and medical isotope production facilities from the use of HEU to the use of low enriched uranium (LEU) fuels and targets, and removal of excess HEU and separated plutonium. The Request also provides $337 million for Global Material Security to build international capacity to secure, and prevent smuggling of, nuclear and radiological material through equipment installations and upgrades, and capacity-building workshops and trainings. In addition, the Request provides $125 million for the Nonproliferation and Arms Control program to strengthen the nonproliferation and arms control regimes by enhancing international nuclear safeguards; controlling the spread of nuclear material, equipment, technology, and expertise; and verifying nuclear reductions and compliance with nonproliferation and arms control treaties and agreements.

Advancing Navy Nuclear Propulsion

Finally for NNSA, the Naval Reactors program continues its tradition of providing the design, development and operational support required to provide militarily effective nuclear propulsion plants and ensure their safe, reliable and long-lived operation. In carrying out this mission, the Naval Reactors program has marked many major accomplishments.

The program continues to provided technical support and 24/7 reachback support for the Navy's nuclear fleet of 73 submarines and 10 aircraft carriers. The program successfully achieved criticality in the first reactor of the new Gerald R. Ford-class aircraft carrier, and continued reactor plant design for the Ohio-class submarine replacement and advanced technology development in refueling of S8G land-based prototype reactor, including the insertion of new materials and technology for the Ohio-class submarine replacement. Naval Reactors also operated the MARF (Modifications and Additions to a Reactor Facility) and S8G land-based prototype reactors, delivering 2,832 trained nuclear operators to the fleet—a 17 percent increase over FY 2014.

The Request includes $1.4 billion for Naval Reactors, an increase of $45 million from the FY 2016 level, to support U.S. Navy nuclear propulsion. The Request provides $214 million to continue development of the Ohio-class submarine replacement reactor, and $124 million to continue refueling of the Land-Based Prototype reactor.

In support of necessary facilities for handling naval spent nuclear fuel, including the capability to receive, unload, prepare, and package naval spent nuclear fuel, the Request provides $100 million to complete design and initiate construction of a new Spent Fuel Handling Recapitalization Project at Naval Reactors Facility in Idaho.

Management and Performance

The FY 2017 Budget Request provides $6.8 billion for Departmental management, performance, and related corporate support activities to position the Department to meet the nation's Manhattan Project and Cold War legacy responsibilities and to continue institutionalizing an enterprise-wide focus on improving the efficiency and effectiveness of DOE programs through the effective management of DOE's infrastructure and workforce.

Strengthening Project Management

The Department is aggressively pursuing implementation of a Secretarial initiative to improve project management. We have made progress to that end through several recent initiatives and reforms, including establishing independent project review capabilities within each Under Secretary organization, as well as a central Project Management Risk Committee (PMRC). We have also formalized the role of the Energy Systems Acquisition Advisory Board (ESAAB) and instituted process changes to ensure that the ESAAB takes a proactive role in reviewing major projects. In addition, we established a new independent office on project management oversight and assessments.

It is notable the Government Accountability Office (GAO) has narrowed the focus of its watch list to DOE's major projects, and we continue to work towards improving our implementation of those projects. The Department's continuing goal is to control costs to within 10 percent of the baseline estimate for at least 90 percent of our construction projects.

The FY 2017 Budget Request includes several proposals to further implement these project management improvements. The Request provides $18 million for the independent office of Project Management Oversight and Assessments (PMOA). With senior management focus on DOE's total project portfolio, DOE will be able to hold contractors and programs accountable for large and at-risk projects, receiving early warning notifications and quarterly updates.

The Budget Request also includes $5 million to establish an independent office, similar to that at the Department of Defense, to set cost estimating policy and provide timely unbiased program evaluation analysis and cost estimation.

Cleaning up Nuclear Legacy Waste

The FY 2017 Budget Request includes $6.1 billion for Environmental Management (EM), $99 million below the FY 2016 enacted level, to address its responsibilities for the cleanup of large quantities of liquid radioactive waste, spent nuclear fuel, contaminated soil and groundwater, and deactivating and decommissioning excess facilities used by the nation's nuclear weapons program. The $6.1 billion Request includes $5.4 billion in discretionary funding and proposes $674 million in mandatory funding from the USEC Fund, for Uranium Enrichment Decontamination and Decommissioning (UED&D) Fund activities.

While difficult challenges lie ahead with some of our remaining Environmental Management projects, it is important to note that when the program started, there were 107 sites to be closed—and today we have cleaned up all but 16 sites. The remaining sites will not be simple to remediate, but we started with over 3,000 square miles to remediate, and only 300 square miles remain.

In our ongoing efforts to remediate our legacy sites, we have continued construction activities necessary to initiate direct feed of Low Activity Waste (LAW) at Hanford, and we have continued technical issue resolution of the Pretreatment and High Level Waste facilities at the same site. We have cleaned up and demolished more than 800 facilities at Hanford, and we have remediated over 1,200 waste sites along the River Corridor. At the Savannah River Site, we have closed the seventh waste tank, and we have revitalized the EM Technology Development and Deployment Program in response to a Secretary of Energy Advisory Board (SEAB) recommendation.

Looking forward, the FY 2017 Budget Request includes $271 million to maintain critical progress toward resuming waste emplacement in the underground at the Waste Isolation Pilot Plant (WIPP) by the end of 2016. WIPP, the Nation's only mined geologic repository for the permanent disposal of defense-generated transuranic waste, suspended operations following a February 5, 2014 fire involving an underground vehicle and an unrelated radioactive release that occurred February 14, 2014. The Request for WIPP includes activities to resume waste emplacement operations by the end of 2016, including continued implementation of corrective actions and safety management program improvements, completion of Operational Readiness Reviews and commencement of waste emplacement operations. Activities include mine stabilization, mining, mine habitability activities in all underground areas, continued decontamination of contaminated areas, and upgrades, support for completion of repairs of New Mexico Roads used for the transportation of DOE shipments of transuranic waste to WIPP, and community and regulatory support. The budget supports the Central Characterization Project and maintains shipping capability between the generator sites and WIPP. The Request also includes funding to support progress in design of a new permanent ventilation system that is needed to support normal operations.

The FY 2017 Budget Request provides $1.5 billion for the Office of River Protection, $86 million above the FY 2016 enacted level, to support the Department's proposal to amend the Consent Decree between DOE and the State of Washington for completion of the Waste Treatment and Immobilization Plant and retrieval of waste from 19 Single Shell Tanks. The Budget Request would enable construction of a new facility to allow DOE to begin treating low level waste by the end of 2022, avoiding the need to wait for completion of other facilities affected by the technical issues. The Request continues construction of the low activity waste (LAW) facility, the analytical laboratory, and balance of facilities while addressing technical issues with the pretreatment facility and the high-level waste facility as well as support for the planning and design of the LAW pretreatment system at the tank farms.

The Request also provides $800 million for cleanup of the Richland Site. Cleanup activities include soil and groundwater remediation, facility decontamination and decommissioning, stabilization and disposition of nuclear materials and spent nuclear fuel, and disposition of waste other than the tank waste managed by the

Office of River Protection. The FY 2017 Request for Richland will provide for continued achievement of important cleanup progress required by the Tri-Party Agreement. The Budget Request for Richland supports completion of cleanup at the Plutonium Finishing Plant, planning and initiation of procurement in preparation for cleanup of the 324 site, and other activities. The decrease of $191 million from FY 2016 is attributed to completed scope and facility modifications to prepare for installation of sludge removal systems for the K West Basin, as well as purchase of the engineered containers for sludge repackaging; and completion of remediation in the 300 area, 100K area and 618-10 trenches.

The Request provides $1.5 billion, $111 million above FY 2016, for the Savannah River Site to support remaining construction and commissioning of the Salt Waste Processing Facility, processing 19 million gallons of salt waste and nuclear materials in H-Canyon, and site-wide infrastructure. The Request will ramp up commissioning of the Salt Waste Processing Facility to enable start-up in 2018. The Request devotes significant funding to support the Liquid Tank Waste Management Program, as the liquid waste tanks pose the highest public, worker, and environmental risk at the site. The Request also supports the Savannah River Site to operate H Canyon in a safe and secure manner, provides safe, secure storage for spent (used) nuclear fuel in L-Area, and supports continuity of K-Area operations to include maintaining K-Area to store special nuclear material safely and securely. The increase over FY 2016 provides additional support leading to startup of Salt Waste Processing Facility in 2018; supports tank closure and bulk waste removal activities to meet FY 2016 enforceable milestones; and provides additional funding for Salt Disposal Unit #7 design activities.

The FY 2017 Budget Request includes $370 million, $32 million below FY 2016, for the Idaho Site to support key requirements to continue progress in meeting the Idaho Settlement Agreement commitments. The Idaho Cleanup Project is responsible for the treatment, storage, and disposition of a variety of radioactive and hazardous waste streams, including removal and disposition of targeted buried waste sitting above the Snake River Plain Aquifer. The project is also responsible for removing or deactivating unneeded facilities, and removing DOE's inventory of spent (used) nuclear fuel and high-level waste from Idaho. The Request will continue retrieval and processing of transuranic waste via the Advanced Mixed Waste Treatment Project and the Remote-handled Waste Disposition Project. It will also support continued progress toward closing the tank farm, including continued treatment and disposition of sodium bearing waste and progress toward buried waste exhumation under the Accelerated Retrieval Project. The decrease from the FY 2016 level is attributed to progress in treatment, packaging, and certification of Idaho Settlement Agreement remote-handled transuranic waste, delays in processing waste at the Integrated Waste Treatment Unit, and a one-time funding increase in FY 2016 for procurements.

The FY 2017 Budget Request provides $391 million for cleanup at the Oak Ridge site, including $178 million in proposed mandatory funding, to support direct shipments of Uranium Solidification Project material, continue design and construction of the Mercury Treatment Facility, continue contact- and remote-handled debris processing at the Transuranic Waste Processing Facility, and continue the K-27 Decontamination and Decommissioning project. The Request will maintain the facilities in a safe, compliant, and secure manner as well as operate waste management facilities. The Request will continue development of Comprehensive Environmental Response, Compensation and Liability Act documentation for the new On-Site Disposal Facility. The processing of legacy transuranic waste debris will continue at the Transuranic Waste Processing Center and technology maturation and design will continue for the Sludge Processing Facility Buildout project. Additionally, the Request supports direct disposition of Consolidated Edison Uranium Solidification Project material from Building 3019, assuming resolution of stakeholder concerns.

The Budget Request includes $323 million, including $258 million in proposed mandatory funding, to support the deactivation and decommissioning project at the Portsmouth Gaseous Diffusion Plant in Piketon, Ohio. In addition to supporting deactivation and decommissioning of gaseous diffusion plant facilities and systems, disposal of waste, small equipment removal, and other related activities, the request also includes funding for design and construction of a potential on-site landfill for the disposal of waste generated from the demolition of the Portsmouth Gaseous Diffusion Plant and associated facilities. In addition, the Request will continue the safe operation of the DUF6 Conversion facility that converts depleted uranium hexafluoride into a more stable depleted uranium oxide form suitable for reuse or disposition. The Request for the Portsmouth is supplemented by continuing transfers of uranium for cleanup services at the Portsmouth Gaseous Diffusion Plant.

The Request provides $272 million for the Paducah site, including $208 million in proposed mandatory funding, for a multifaceted portfolio of processing and cleanup activities. In addition to ongoing environmental cleanup and DUF6 operations, the Budget Request supports activities to continue the environmental remediation and further stabilize the gaseous diffusion plant, including uranium deposit removal, facility modifications, surveillance and maintenance, and activities to remove hazardous materials. The Request supports the design of the Paducah potential On-Site Waste Disposal Facility project, if the project is selected as the appropriate remedy.

The FY 2017 Budget Request includes $30 million to expand the technology development program through carefully targeted projects to develop and demonstrate new technologies and approaches tailored to the specific contamination issues at individual sites. The FY 2017 Budget Request includes an emphasis on robotics research and development of test beds in support of DOE's cleanup mission.

Refinancing Uranium Enrichment Decontamination and Decommissioning

Continued progress towards decontaminating, decommissioning, and remediating the former gaseous diffusion uranium enrichment sites, and towards meeting our uranium/thorium reimbursement commitments, remains a priority for DOE. We have made significant strides at the Oak Ridge, Portsmouth, and Paducah sites, but we have an estimated $22-24 billion in remaining cleanup costs.

Throughout the history of these sites, the government has collected funds from the public and private entities that utilized the enriched uranium produced at the facilities to pay for operation, privatization, and cleanup of these three sites—some provided by utility fees, and others provided by Congress. Three government accounts— Uranium Enrichment Decontamination and Decommissioning Fund, Uranium Supply and Enrichment Activities Account, and the United States Enrichment Corporation (USEC) Fund—hold nearly $5 billion of these funds.

The FY 2017 Budget Request proposes to make progress on our cleanup missions at Paducah, Portsmouth, and Oak Ridge, and the Title X Uranium/Thorium Reimbursement Program by harnessing some of these funds through a mandatory proposal to make available $674 million from the United States Enrichment Corporation Fund.

Through the Energy Policy Act of 1992, Congress authorized annual deposits to the Uranium Enrichment Decontamination and Decommissioning (UED&D) Fund from an assessment on nuclear utilities for 15 years—from fiscal years 1993 through 2007. The Budget Request proposes to reinstate these fees to offset proposed new mandatory spending for uranium enrichment cleanup. The Budget also includes $155 million of defense funding for deposit into the UED&D Fund, reflecting the shared responsibility of both industry and the federal government for these costs.

Investing in Departmental Infrastructure

The FY 2017 Budget Request supports safe and reliable world class facilities by investing in new infrastructure in all mission areas and establishing a sustainable trajectory for the Department's existing infrastructure.

As part of our effort to manage the enterprise's infrastructure in a sustainable manner to support DOE missions, beginning in FY 2016, we have implemented a policy to halt increases in deferred maintenance across the DOE complex. We have also taken steps to bolster DOE's enterprise-wide inventory by compiling the first uniform assessment of general purpose infrastructure at all National Laboratories and NNSA plants and sites through the National Laboratory Operations Board (LOB), and forming a LOB working group to assess and prioritize the disposition of excess facilities.

Building on these efforts, the FY 2017 Budget Request continues a comprehensive program of infrastructure modernization and improved maintenance across the complex, including expanded funding for general purpose infrastructure projects. The Budget proposes, for example, $200 million for the disposal of the Kansas City Bannister Federal complex. Finally, we are seeking to improve the energy efficiency and sustainability of government facilities, including use of Energy Savings Performance Contracts.

Building and Supporting the Energy Workforce

DOE's continues to work to attract, manage, train and retain the best workforce to meet its future mission needs.

In support of managing the workforce and hiring new personnel, we have activated two Consolidated Human Resources (HR) Service Centers, at Cincinnati and Oak Ridge, as part of a new service delivery model to consolidate 17 current HR service centers to five, which should allow for a more efficient and effective HR model across DOE. The FY 2017 Budget Request completes the HR Shared Services Centers consolidation and invests in implementing recommendations resulting from a talent management study conducted in FY 2016, which will help to develop a corporate approach to talent acquisition in order to consistently and effectively attract, develop, and retain the best workforce to meet mission needs.

The DOE Office of the Chief Information Officer (CIO) and related offices continue to build the information technology (IT) infrastructure in support of DOE's mission needs. DOE is expanding Multifactor Authentication Program for improved cyber security. The FY 2017 Budget Request strengthens cybersecurity across the enterprise with an investment of $285 million, an increase of $23 million across 13 offices and the Working Capital Fund.

The $93 million FY 2017 Budget Request for CIO, $20 million above FY 2016, also supports several critical IT improvements, including implementation of Federal Information Technology Acquisition Reform Act (FITARA) requirements to provide a common baseline for roles, responsibilities, requirements, and authorities for the management of IT in federal civilian agencies. The Request also includes efforts to modernize and further secure the Department's IT infrastructure, including core networking layers, data centers, and access technologies.

The Department has established a Labor-Management Forum to further encourage opportunities for collaboration and partnership between contractors and management.

The Department has established the Office of Energy Jobs Development, consolidating ongoing activities across the Department formerly coordinated via the Jobs Strategy Council. The Request includes $3.7 million to support the office and to compile survey data and deliver the energy jobs and workforce report that would detail job growth/shifts in the energy and advanced manufacturing industries; fill the gaps that currently exist in data gathering on renewable energy, energy efficiency, and advanced manufacturing jobs; and compile data on energy job skill needs of employers and public agencies.

Advancing DOE's Critical Missions

In conclusion, the FY 2017 Budget Request of $32.5 billion invests in its science and technology capabilities, its workforce, and its critical infrastructure to advance DOE's core missions.

The Request supports the Department's efforts in science and energy to enable a clean energy future through innovative lower-cost energy technologies; to support secure, modern and resilient energy infrastructure and emergency response capabilities; and to provide the backbone for discovery and innovation, especially in the physical sciences, for America's research community.

The Request invests in the Department's nuclear security missions to maintain a safe, secure, and effective nuclear deterrent without nuclear explosive testing; to modernize the nuclear security research and production infrastructure; to reduce global nuclear security threats; and to propel our nuclear Navy.

And the Request continues taking steps to further the Department's management and performance missions to clean up from the Cold War legacy of nuclear weapons production; to manage infrastructure in a sustainable manner to support DOE missions; and to attract, manage, train and retain the best workforce to meet mission needs.

Thank you, and I would be pleased to answer your questions.